Why Driveway on Fire?
Parenting Your Teens and Tweens

To Kara,
God bless you —
It's fun working w/ you!
— Cynthia

Cynthia Gill, MA, LMFT

outskirts
press

Why is the Driveway on Fire?
Parenting Your Teens and Tweens
All Rights Reserved.
Copyright © 2021 Cynthia Gill, MA, LMFT
v2.0

The opinions expressed in this manuscript are solely the opinions of the author and do not represent the opinions or thoughts of the publisher. The author has represented and warranted full ownership and/or legal right to publish all the materials in this book.

This book may not be reproduced, transmitted, or stored in whole or in part by any means, including graphic, electronic, or mechanical without the express written consent of the publisher except in the case of brief quotations embodied in critical articles and reviews.

Outskirts Press, Inc.
http://www.outskirtspress.com

ISBN: 978-1-9772-3907-5

Cover Illustration © 2021 Abigail Gill. All rights reserved - used with permission.

Scripture quotations taken from the (NASB®) New American Standard Bible®, Copyright © 1960, 1971, 1977, 1995, 2020 by The Lockman Foundation. Used by permission. All rights reserved. www.lockman.org

Outskirts Press and the "OP" logo are trademarks belonging to Outskirts Press, Inc.

PRINTED IN THE UNITED STATES OF AMERICA

Table of Contents

Introduction	i
One: Four Vitals for Raising Confident Kids	1
Two: Encouragement	4
Three: Family Meetings	8
Four: Positive Atmosphere	13
Five: Resolving Conflict with Mutual Respect	17
Six: Entitlement : Let's Beat It	21
Seven: Reflections in a Foggy Mirror	25
Eight: Screen Time (from *Jump-Starting Boys*)	28
Nine: Voice	37
Ten: "I just want to be happy"	40
Eleven: Anxiety	42
Twelve: How to Defeat Depression	46

Thirteen: On Children Leaving the Faith					50

Fourteen: The Number 1 Reason Kids Reject Christianity	56

Fifteen: 8 Simple Prayers that Help Marriages			59

Final Word									62

Resources									63

Acknowledgments								64

Introduction

Little did we know what adventures the 6 teen-age boys (ages 13-15) we took up to the lake that weekend had planned! When we got there, they did the normal things: took out the canoe and sank it, took out the paddleboat and promptly went over to the other side of the lake, so I had to take the canoe over to within shouting distance and tell them to come home. Then they decided to get on their bikes and ride to the corner store.

About ½ hour later, my mother in law, (who raised 5 kids herself) said, "Why is the driveway on fire?"

She said it remarkably calmly. The boys had purchased cans of white gas and matches at the store, and were experimenting with it. Starting fires.

Later we would laugh about it. Not at that moment, however.

That's it, decided my husband. No more passive, sitting around, leaving them to their own devices. "Hey you guys, let's get on our bikes, and ride around the lake!" he proposed. Thankfully, that wore them out (it's a big lake). They fell into bed and slept soundly.

Boys. Teenage boys. Their brains aren't developed yet. Till they're 26 I'm told. The pre-frontal cortex isn't mature yet. No wonder they do such hair-brained things.

Girls do too. Meltdowns. Drama. Hiding things from parents.

It's scary. But, the one thing both boys and girls want is an adult with time. An adult who won't judge them. Who will LISTEN to them. Connect with them. Did you know it only takes one adult who is interested in a teen to help him or her move onto the right path? Or stay on the right path?

This book aims to show you how you can be that person.

ONE

Four Vitals for Raising Confident Kids

Julia (not her real name) was antsy. She had ridden in the car for too many hours, and she was ready to be done. She began to scream, whine, and complain loudly. Her dad, who was driving, got into a verbal sparing with her, which went downhill fast. What's a person to do? Thankfully, grandma was in the back seat, and decided to engage Julia in a conversation. "What are you looking forward to this summer?" she asked.

The atmosphere changed immediately. Julia turned from an angry, snarling animal into a sweet, lively child. She and grandma had a good conversation.

In our book on parenting, we use an acrostic, LOVE, to describe what young people need: **L**isten, **O**rder, **V**oice, and **E**mpathy.

In our haste to get things done, as parents, we do not **listen** very well. If we are to raise the next generation to be healthy, confident individuals, this needs to change. Every person, and especially your child, needs to know that someone cares about what they think. When your child says something outrageous, you can respond in one of two ways. You can shut the child down, berating him either or by attitude or by words, such as, "You are stupid!" Or, you can listen, and affirm his worth. "I can hear that you are really frustrated with your teacher," is an example of active listening. This technique acknowledges the child's *emotions* behind her *statements*.

Too often we focus on the content of what they're saying and we argue with that. This does not connect with the child's heart, and usually puts both parties on the *defensive*. Because the parent is usually bigger, more articulate, and smarter, the parent usually "wins." But in power struggles, who really wins? *Do you want to be right, or be effective?*

<u>Order</u> means that the child is not in charge. Listening and giving the child a voice does NOT mean they get their way all the time! Anarchy brings much insecurity. In families where the children reign supreme, where parents cater to their every whim, children are very discouraged. Often these children are the ones who exhibit the "failure to launch" problems. When parents exhibit a quiet confidence that they are in charge, the children will sense that. If, however, the parents try to maintain order by using anger and threats, the children will react with fear, and trust will not grow. In that case, the order will be superficial, masking an inner chaos in the child's heart. Provide guidance with a mixture of firmness and gentleness.

<u>Voice</u> Every person has a voice, but not all voices are heard. *Teens may say outrageous things, because their pre-frontal cortex is not developed yet!* But it is crucial that you hear them out. Otherwise they internalize their (wrong) perceptions, repeat them to themselves over and over again, and they will come out later. Ask them how and what questions to challenge them. For example, if they say they are going to drop out of high school, say "Hmm, interesting. How is that going to work for you when you try to get a job?"

FOUR VITALS FOR RAISING CONFIDENT KIDS

Let them pontificate, and think of it as puffs of steam that blow away. Let them know you heard them, and maybe you don't agree with them. Ask, "do you want to hear what successful people do?" Then give them a choice. Say they are failing Math. "They might get help from a tutor, or go in early for help from the teacher. Which one of these things would work for you?" Giving a teen voice is essential for their development. You are NOT agreeing with what they say, but you are listening to them. *Building dignity in them.*

Empathy is the most appropriate response when a child or young person is angry. Yet parents, in their zeal to correct, often teach children to stifle their emotions. Youth learn to please their parents with their external actions, while on the inside they are seething mad. No wonder they resort to negative behaviors like starving themselves, cutting, or threatening to take their own lives! Think how much better it could be if parents are patient and empathize with the child's pain. Parents may need to be vulnerable, to share with their children their own struggles as they guide them into adulthood with kindness, patience, and firmness.

Effective parenting requires empathy. **Empathy** is only released through **listening**. The answer to our hurting young people is to give them a **voice** and choices. Impart confidence that there is **order** in the world, rather than the despair that comes from shaming them.

But it is worth it! By **listening**, nurturing **order** in children's hearts, giving them a **voice**, and responding with **empathy**, we might be able to spare more families the pain and sorrow that suffering families go through.

Let more of your stories end like Julia's above. You can make a difference, one conversation at a time.

TWO

Encouragement

"It was really out of our comfort zone to go on the Metro with people we didn't know," commented one of my students, upon debriefing after we had taken a trip to Germany and Prague. The students had gone for the night with some friends of ours, and it never occurred to me that they would be scared to travel with them to their homes.

"I didn't like having to go to the bathroom outdoors," said another. Another surprise for me. Wasn't an overseas trip for high schoolers supposed to stretch them, and let them have new experiences?

Teens need encouragement like a plant needs water. Without it, they will dry up and wither.

Encouragement.

The very word conjures up good feelings, as everyone can relate to the need for it in our own experience. Who hasn't felt discouraged at times? I am writing this focus on our youth, who desperately need encouragement in order to grow. Parents have a tremendous amount of power over their children. God planned it that way. Yet, how often we feel at a loss when it comes to nurturing out teenagers and training them in the way that they should go!

Sometimes people get the concept of encouragement mixed up with flattery or compliments. Flattery is negative, the scripture speaks to it: "He who flatters his neighbor is spreading a net for his steps." (Proverbs 29:5) Usually flattery is given with a desire for secondary gain by the flatterer. Parents are not immune to this. Compliments are usually a blessing, when young people can sense they are sincere.

If a person compliments their teen, say on making a goal in a soccer game, that is good.

But the message is also sent that encouragement depends on the young person's performance. What if he/she doesn't make any more goals? For this reason, I believe that the most powerful forms of encouragement are not simply compliments on behavior, although these are certainly appropriate.

True and lasting encouragement looks at the **character** of the individual. Perhaps noticing how kind he/she is to the team member that is not doing well. Or the self-control he/she showed when the other kids were yelling mean things to a kid who messed up and lost the game for them. Or the effort it took to make the goal, to get the A, to make the basket. Praising **effort** is much better than praising the end result.

Christians know that character qualities are longer lasting than any gifts a person might have. Getting in the habit of pointing out and encouraging our kids for their godly character traits will produce confident, loving children. After all, character is a matter of **choice.** Kids who choose character will be forever blessed. Let's encourage them to do so, and model it for them ourselves.

In their landmark book <u>Parenting Teens with Love and Logic</u>, Foster Cline and Jim Fay identify three difference parent styles that they have observed in their work with families.

The first is the "**Helicopter**" parents. These parents hover over their children, wanting to protect them from mistakes, harm, and the harsh realities of today's world. Unfortunately, this is not very encouraging to the child. The message being communicated is "You cannot handle this on your own, you need me at all times." So the young person grows up discouraged, and lacking confidence. This may be manifested in a variety of ways, from depression to smoldering anger.

A second style of parenting is the "**Drill Sergeant.**" In a militaristic way, these parents give orders to their children, allowing no discussion, compromise, or negotiation. Listening is not part of the process in this style. Such children may obey for a while, but inside they are very discouraged. They believe that they are not capable of making decisions on their own, and thus grow up looking for others to do their thinking for them. They also may react in anger after they leave home, or act out in a variety of other ways even beforehand.

The third type of parent is the "**Consultant.**" These wise parents talk with their teen and most importantly listen to them. They help their teen to explore the consequences of foolish choices, and express their confidence that the teen will make the right choices. The teen feels respected, affirmed, and encouraged. When the teen senses that the parent is sincere, he or she will rise to the occasion, and live out that expectation. Wise parents make sure consequences are in place so the teen will learn from any mistakes they make along the way.

Raising teenagers is not for the faint of heart! But raising confident young people who are learning how to think for themselves based on truth is vital in today's world. There is currently a war going on in our culture. The winners will get our children.

Maybe I didn't prepare my students well enough for the new experiences they would be having on the above-mentioned European trip. Hmmmm, I'm still learning at my age.

THREE

Family Meetings

When I was growing up, a "family meeting" was only held if there was something wrong. It was usually a boring time of Dad or Mom lecturing us. When my husband and I were raising our kids, we did the same thing. Only after the kids left home did I find out what a REAL family meeting was!

Whatever age your children are, everyone can benefit from family meetings. In well-run family meetings, children learn three things: (a) that their *voice* is important, (b) that collaborative *problem-solving* works, and (c) that the skill of *encouragement* is a vital component (some say the most important) in maintaining healthy relationships. Such skills are a vital part of growing up, yet there seems to be a dearth of these skills today. The good news is that it is not too late to begin implementing them.

Let's starts with the third, and arguably one of the most important skills: encouragement. It is very appropriate for families to sit down and ask each member to state one positive quality about the others. For maximum benefit, choose a character quality rather than a comment on the appearance or talent of the person. "I appreciate this about mom...about dad...about Mary...about Joe..." Such an activity will start the family meeting off on the right foot, with a positive focus. Who doesn't like to hear something good about themselves?

Then it is time to solve a problem together. Perhaps there is a problem that affects the whole family, for example: "The dog needs to go out at 7 a.m. on Saturdays and everyone wants to sleep in. How can we solve this?" Each person needs to be able to express their voice, without interruption or fear of ridicule. No matter how outrageous the solution that a family member suggests, ("I think Dad should get up every Saturday!") it is very important that all treat it with respect. ("That won't work for Dad, but we appreciate your sharing, Jonny!")

Skills of *negotiation, self expression, listening, and compromise* are taught as the family interacts, with the goal of reaching a mutually acceptable solution. Explaining "Well, that won't work for me" when one child suggests dad get up every Saturday at 7, models negotiation and *assertiveness* skills.

Brainstorming is a very valuable skill to teach, just be sure you don't stifle it by judging each suggestion as it is comes out. If someone suggests that they have candy at every meal, Mom or Dad's response can be "Now what do you think my thoughts are about that? Will that work for me?"

Two dangers lurk in the background, threatening to hijack the collaborative problem solving process. The first is inability to listen. Active listening needs to be taught! Most of us are not good at truly listening. We are already formulating our response, even before the other one is finished speaking! The only way to learn this is to calm ourselves, and require that people say "I heard you say..."and then reflect back what they heard. This will take time to learn!

The other danger is one person (often the parent) talking too much, dominating the meeting. After all parents know it all, right? Then, they end up talking **at** the children, and no one benefits. Parents, you can be right, or you can be effective. I would urge you to choose the latter, and thus model mutual respect.

If you decide to have weekly family, meetings, be patient. Perhaps they will only last 15 minutes if you have young children. You may not always arrive at a mutually acceptable solution. Keep on trying. Educate yourselves on the process by looking at the resources below. Your investment will bring returns for your entire life, and likely passed on for many generations to come. Does that sound worthwhile?

In our book *Jump-Starting Boys,* we have the following suggestions.

"An excellent way to improve self-esteem, build character, teach collaborative problem solving, and give children voice is to hold family meetings. Here are several tips for conducting them:

1) Start with appreciations or compliments. Each person tells other family members something they appreciate about them in the past week. *"I appreciate how you helped me with the dinner last night." "I think you were generous when you gave your cookie to Joey."*

2) Choose a topic to discuss and ask for input on how to solve it. *"Let's talk about how to deal with the problem of computer time. How can we stop the fighting that happens after school when everyone wants to use it?"*

3) Each family member takes a turn suggesting solutions to the problem. Treat each other with respect, regardless of whether you agree with their idea.

4) Set ground rules: no interrupting, no put-downs, keep a calm voice. Everyone needs to feel safe and heard. The goal is to solve the problem (if possible) but even more importantly, to teach mutual respect.

5) Brainstorm! This is a valuable skill to teach. Can you collectively come up with eight possible solutions? The key is to refrain from judging or evaluating the potential solutions until you are done brainstorming. It's fun and energizing to let the creative juices flow.

6) If a problem cannot be solved in a meeting, table it until the next one.

7) End the meeting with a treat and a fun activity if possible.

8) Remember, meetings are more effective if you have them every week, not on the parent's whim or only when there is a crisis.

9) Rather than engaging in an argument in the heat of the moment, say, "Let's put this on the agenda for the next family meeting." That gives you and the kids the opportunity to cool down, and they will look forward to being heard. Keep the family meetings a forum for thoughtful discussion.

10) Start and end the meetings on time. Set a timer so the kids know it will not drag on. Keep them short (fifteen minutes if you have preschoolers, twenty to twenty-five minutes maximum if you have teens)."

Try it! Just 15 minutes, once a week for starters. Be persistent, and you'll get lots out of them, once everyone gets used to them.

More on Family meetings are in Jane Nelsen's *Positive Discipline* books.

FOUR

Positive Atmosphere

The green leaves of the trees were blowing in the wind. We were outside enjoying a Minnesota spring, and I asked my teenage granddaughter, Jackie, what she could do to live a life more in line with the way God wants her to live. "Well, I could be more positive," she replied. I was pleasantly surprised. "Of course, we all can!" was my answer.

But later, as I mused over her words, I thought of how profound and yet how simple they were.

Is it possible that bitter chemicals come out of our mouths when we say negative words? I heard a story recently of plants that died when negative words were spoken to them. There were two sets of plants: both with equal amounts of light, water, nutrition, and soil. But the difference was that one had a person speaking negatively: shouting insults, negative words daily at it. The other one had a person speaking kindly to it. Amazingly enough, the one with the positive words thrived, while the other one shriveled up and died!

Now, as a psychologist I know that bitter, mean words change the brain chemicals. And so can positive ones. (Whether they have an effect on plants or not, I'd have to try the experiment myself.)

But what if they do? Or, what if they ONLY affect brain chemicals? So, your brain will be healthier if you speak positively to yourself and others? DUH!

Read the following with this in mind...

Who has the power to "set the thermostat" of the environment in our homes and places of work? WE do! Do we want the atmosphere to be bitter and negative, or healthy, hope-filled? *Parents, our children marinate in the atmosphere of our homes. They are looking to us to see how we cope with the challenges of life!* Following are some tips on maintaining a positive and confidence-building atmosphere:

1) <u>Listen to yourself</u>. How many times do you hear yourself doing one of the big 3 C's:

> *Complaining, Criticizing,* or being *Cynical?* Count how many times you say the word *"frustrated"*, *"annoyed,"* or other such words. What comes out of our mouth is indicative of what is in our hearts, so some time for reflection is in order if we are speaking too much negativity. *Ration for yourself how many times you will allow yourself to express negativity per day.* Cynicism imparts the attitude that we are powerless, research suggests that we CAN actively work to change that. Learned helplessness does not benefit anyone.

2) Develop a <u>supply of positive phrases</u> that you can say to help you *cope* with life's challenges.

> Here are some suggestions to get you started:
>
> "Well, the good things about _____ far outweigh the bad."
>
> "It could be worse. We could live in _____ , where there is no food, medical care, infrastructure, etc."

"If this is the <u>worst</u> thing that happens all day (or all week) that is not TOO bad!"

3) Combat anxiety by <u>speaking truth to yourself</u>.

"What's the *worst case* scenario?" "What would I do in that case?"

"Is anyone going to die?" (if we run out milk today, etc.)

"What is the likelihood of that happening?"

4) List all the positive things that happened today (or this morning, or about this event, in this situation, etc.). Work hard at counting/listing your blessings and giving thanks. This skill is very simple and many have heard it for years. Interestingly enough, it is gaining prestige as one of the "newest" discoveries in the field of psychology!

<u>Thankfulness</u> is a *very valuable weapon* in our quest to defeat anxiety, depression, and "entitlementitis." But it needs to be intentional, and it is taught best by example. Rather than preaching at someone "you should be more thankful," list things YOU are grateful for, and then ask them to follow your example.

5) <u>Quiet yourself</u>. Take a few minutes to meditate on something of beauty and wonder, it will change your perspective. *A quiet heart can receive from God.* In our noisy culture we forget the power of stillness. Some call it the "gentle whisper" or "still small voice." Peace and a hopeful attitude simply will not happen if we are constantly allowing ourselves to be bombarded with external stimuli, including screens! Addiction to screens creates a climate for anxiety to skyrocket.

Whether we are raising children, or working in another setting, perhaps with no children around, we will have a higher quality of life if we learn to be more positive. Far from being a "Pollyanna," we will have a *quiet confidence* that draws others to us, and commands their respect.

Does the world need such qualities?

Yes, Jackie, we can all be more positive. Let's do it!

FIVE

Resolving Conflict with Mutual Respect

Joey was exasperated. "What, another family fight? Why can't we just get along?" It seemed like the family was always arguing, and nothing ever got resolved.

I can't think of too many things more essential than to teach conflict resolution skills to our families.

Often family members come to me as a professional counselor for reconciliation: parents and adult children, spouses working on their relationship, and teens with their parents are the most common. In almost every situation I find a single element missing: **mutual respect.**

All parties are discouraged, angry, and pointing the finger of blame at the others. How can we avoid this, or if it applies to us, engage in communication that *is effective so we can find reconciliation?*

Here are some guidelines that can help people better resolve conflict:

1. Speak with respect and calmness, rather than <u>preaching, teaching</u>, or angrily trying to change the other person's beliefs

through argument. Here is an example of a harsh start up: The teen has planned a graduation event on his little brother's birthday. (_Sarcastically_) "_Thanks a lot for planning a graduation party on Jonny's birthday! You should think of the rest of the family before you make your plans!_" Here is an example of more respectful or softer start up. "_Honey, did you forget it is Jonny's birthday in 2 weeks when you organized that graduation party? I really want you here at his party, so does he, and I feel hurt by this. How can we solve this thing together?_"

2. Speak directly and honestly, rather than hinting or assuming. Ask to check out your conclusions rather than assuming. In the second example, the speaker is not assuming bad motives on the teen's part.

3. Be cordial, respectful, even if you disagree, rather than insulting or accusing the other one. The first example above might continue: "_I can't believe how selfish you are, only thinking of your own pleasure rather than the family, or even your own little brother! You're going to be just like your good-for-nothing father, a dead-beat dad._" A much better way would be: "_I am guessing you really do want to be here for his party, right? Would it work to re-schedule your graduation party for another day? Do you have any other ideas? I really think it is very important!_"

4. Avoid name-calling, emotional outbursts with profanity, and the use of always and never. "_You jerk, you always ignore your brother's needs!_"

5. Keep emotional distance, which means choose not to get drawn into reacting emotionally. Soothe yourself with self-calming techniques like deep breathing or taking a time out. "_I am feeling so frustrated right now, I need about 20 minutes to cool down. Can we talk again in 20 minutes?_"

6. Be ready to admit your part in the conflict, ask forgiveness. John Gottman calls these "repair attempts", and observes that in healthy relationships, both parties stay on the alert to make and accept them. Here are some examples: *"Well, maybe I was over-reacting. I need to calm down. Your point of view does make sense, can we compromise?"*

Avoiding the underlined terms above will only work if we are able to manage our anger, however. How many times have we experienced what Daniel Siegel calls "emotional hi-jacking," where we have the best of intentions, but then someone pushes our hot button? We react, and set the process back by saying things we later regret. Sadly, the rational mind seems to shut down when the emotions are activated. So, self-soothing skills are vital if we are to conduct family (or any relational) communication. John Gottman in his landmark books urges people to "soothe yourself and each other" as part of the problem-solving process.

Underneath emotional hijacking is a mistaken belief. People believe with all their hearts that they are RIGHT. "Because I am right," the thinking goes, "I need to make my point, and if the other one will listen to me and see it my way, then we can go on." Does this sound familiar? I often say to both parties *"You are both right!"* The question that we need to ask ourselves is "Do I want to be right or to be effective?" Do I want the relationship, or to be right?" *"Do I want to be RIGHT or be restored?"* Often the solution is found not in who is right and who is wrong but in how we can function together.

Choose a few of the above pointers, think about them, and apply them to yourself personally. After all, you can't change the other person, but you can change yourself.

Yes, Joey, you CAN get along, but we need to learn the skills. Like playing soccer: learn the skills! It's worth it.

Here are some resources for additional reading:

http://www.amazon.com/Daniel-J.-Siegel/e/B00459LSPI#
http://emotioncoaching.gottman.com/
http://www.gottman.com/about-us-2/dr-john-gottman/

SIX

Entitlement : Let's Beat It

"Daddy, will you get me a pencil?" asked Becky. Daddy immediately put down his coffee, and went over to the table, retrieved the pencil, and handed it to the girl. I thought, 'Hmmmm, why couldn't she get that herself?" "Dad, I need some more paper," whined Becky.

What's a parent to do? Say "how high?" whenever your kid says "jump?" NO! Read the following to see what the result is when we do for kids what *they can do for themselves*.

    A. Praising problems

        1. Praising what takes *no effort*. Rewards and praise are most effective when they focus on an achievement that took time and energy.

        2. Praising for what is *required*. Everyone has things that are expected of them, praising them for all sorts of little things creates "praise inflation."

        3. Praising what is *not specific*. "You are amazing!" Praise should go in one of 4 buckets: hard work, being kind, being

honest, being vulnerable. Non-specific, excessive statements have no bucket, so they are either not believed, or go towards making the child more narcissistic.

4. Praising and telling your child that he/she is *better than others*. "You deserve special treatment" instead of "You worked hard with your team and your individual plays were excellent. Now go and help your coach pick up the equipment." A wise man said once, "He who ignores discipline despises himself." (Proverbs 15:32)

5. Praising *not based on reality*. "You can do anything you want to do," is unrealistic, it leads to disappointment and resentment.

6. A *lack of warmth* in a family upbringing. Creates a defensive grandiose identity, who comes across as arrogant and superior.

7. Praise the *character* in a person rather than always the achievement. This points out that the person has made a choice to do right, regardless of their talent or lack thereof.

Loving but firm is a key. Boundaries must be set and enforced to show the person the balance between grace and truth.

B. <u>Chores</u> are a good way to beat entitlement. Here are the ABC's of chores:

1. Assign every member of the family some meaningful contributions. Ask yourself: "What am I doing that my kids could do?" Some families find it useful to post the list of contributions on the fridge with the person's name next to it. Note- don't say "Do it now," or you will be inviting power struggles. Simply give them a deadline.

2. Be quiet! Don't nag.

3. Consequences preceded by empathy will teach them. If they refuse, forget, or do a sloppy job, have them repay you for your energy. After all, how much effort did you put forth to do the thing for them? Ideas are: they could do extra chores for you; they could stay home or lose a privilege to save you energy; or they could pay a professional (or you) to do the chores. (Example: when a teenage girl had to pay a maid for doing her chores!)

Daddy and Mommy learned that they should not do for kids what they can do for themselves. It changed their family, and Becky and the other kids became more grown up, more respectful, and more fun!

SEVEN

Reflections in a Foggy Mirror

Gone are the days of sitting by the lake fishing, and just thinking. Far in the past memories of the older generation are the lazy days of walking along, reflecting on life. Everyone is on their screens! "I'm too busy!" How often do we hear or think this?

Our mirrors of life are foggy. Reflecting is becoming a lost art.

But is this healthy? Can we think about something carefully or rationally, and reach a conclusion well without it? My observation is that young people and kids already have lost or are losing the ability to think critically. To think for themselves. To worship. And with these losses come anxiety. A lack of peacefulness.

So what can we do? Do we just sit idly by, and let ourselves be hijacked by our phones and i-pads?

The rebel in me screams "NO!"

Here is a list of questions we can ask ourselves and others to help us learn to think deeply again. Ask yourself these questions. I find that as I'm falling asleep at night, it helps to go over the day this way. Especially "what am I grateful for?"

What am I grateful for today?

What surprised me today?

What made me sad today?

What made me laugh or smile today?

What was a challenge today?

How was I kind today?

How was I brave today?

What were some pleasures today? (another way of saying what I am grateful for)

How did I fail today? (no shame!!)

Take some time to ask yourself some of these every day. Ask your child, teen, adult child. Incorporate them into your day.

Take some time each day to be off your phone. Even 20-30 minutes is better than none.

If we are not led by our thoughts, we are led by the default: our emotions. This unfortunately leads to chaos. Think about it: when I am led by my emotions, without regard for rational thinking, doesn't it lead to chaos?

I have a picture of a train which I often show my clients. It has "thoughts" as the engine, "beliefs" as the coal car, then "behavior" as a car, and lastly a caboose labeled "feelings." If the train is led by thoughts, that is effective living, if it is led by emotions, that leads to chaos. The idea is to be led by your thoughts, which are (ideally) fed by true beliefs. We don't ignore our feelings, but we shouldn't be led by them.

Yet, if we don't take some time to think, to reflect, I fear our society is headed for trouble. Feelings-led people rarely make good decisions. Think the French Revolution, the Rwandan genocide, and the Hitler rallies. All are examples of people being led by mass emotion.

Let's take time to think, to reflect, to worship. It is what we have been given above the animals.

We need to quiet ourselves and do it!

It'll make life's mirror a little less foggy.

EIGHT

Screen Time
(from *Jump-Starting Boys*)

Media guru James P. Steyer recommends that parents set a limit of two hours a day with exceptions for special agreed-upon events such as election returns, the Super Bowl, and New Year's Eve specials. "Kids often respond well to limits; once they know what they are, they learn to live with them." Some parents allow children to "earn" screen time by reading: for every *hour* of pleasure reading they do, they are allowed *half an hour* of media time. This sends a clear message that reading is valued more than electronic-media time.

If you winced at any of the above statistics, be aware that the American Academy of Pediatrics recommends that parents limit children's total screen time to no more than one to two hours of quality programming per day.

Duffy's advice is to express curiosity about what's happening on their screens, rather than trotting out judgment and lectures; be someone genuinely interested in what he's watching, what it's about, how popular it is in his crowd, and, most important, what he thinks of it. "Teenagers like to be experts and teachers—it fosters their sense of competence," Duffy says. "Show an interest by asking instead of telling."

SCREEN TIME (FROM JUMP-STARTING BOYS)

More than any other generation, today's kids are either out of the home or engaged in isolated activities within the home. By putting a limit on their screen time *and* coaxing them to chat about their activities while they are home (without overdoing it), you can build goodwill and their self-confidence simultaneously.

Of course, before you lay down the law on kids' screen time, look at what you are modeling with your iPhone, iPad, Blackberry, and laptop. Pam recently saw a father plop down on the sofa beside his son, who was into his fourth hour of television that day. *Finally*, she thought: some quality father-son time. But the father pulled out his iPad and proceeded to catch up on work. Sadly, proximity does not qualify as attentiveness.

Perhaps make it a parent/kid challenge: Pin a chart on the wall with both yours and the kids' names over columns that track screen time. Use it to cut back screen hours simultaneously. Maybe even provide a family electronic-device drop-box at the front door for certain hours of the day—at least for dinnertime.

A school librarian who started up a boys' reading club was curious when he noticed that the majority of boys who signed up for it were from one large extended family in the community. He asked the parents why all these boys were such keen readers; their answer: "We have strict limits on screen time."

Darian, a former reluctant reader we interviewed, remembers losing interest in reading at around age ten. About the same time, he would rise at seven each morning and sneak down to the basement den to watch television before anyone was up. One day, he arrived to find a lock on the television. It turned out his parents were concerned about his slackening interest in reading and schoolwork.

"It took a couple of days, but I was determined, and I eventually managed to pick the lock," he says proudly. Even so, he got the message, and eventually returned to reading.

"Our family didn't have a formal reading hour or anything," Darian told us, "but from the youngest age, I remember my parents would let me gather my stuffed toys around me, and then we'd make up stories about them. We did that on camping trips too, and I remember it being a really nice thing. Also, I remember a particular teacher who would read aloud to us. She was very good with her voice, and I found my imagination could run more freely when I was being read to, than when the strain of reading distracted me. Anyway, you can only read for so many hours of the day, while listening to words is second nature once you're comfortable."

Sometimes the screen-versus-reading tug-of-war isn't kids' interest in what's on so much as busy, distracted parents giving in without really meaning to, and without realizing the implications. Many parents subscribe to one of the following statements, which we've followed up with a reality-check thought.

"I can't get them off of there." (Said with shrug of surrender.)

Yes you can, and yes, you must if you don't want an underachieving boy. (We offer tips on how to do so in Chapter Seven.) There's also a checklist in Steyer's *The Other Parent*, and excellent information in Jane Healy's *Your Child's Growing Mind* and Nelsen's *Positive Parenting*.

Limit screen time to the widely recommended maximum of two hours per day, with exceptions for agreed-upon specials.

Allow your child to earn more screen time through reading. This sends the message that reading is more important than screen time in your family.

No screens in the bedroom for elementary children. It can adversely affect brain development. Technology is all but robbing younger people of their ability to concentrate and learn.

Check labels of games and movies for age recommendations and stick to them.

Password protect your computer, lock your TV, or whatever else it takes to enforce your limits.

When possible, "co-watch" programs and "co-listen" to music lyrics with your children, and when you come across objectionable material, ask them what they think about it. Rather than lecture them, ask them for permission to give your opinion, or say, "What do you think I am thinking right now?" Research shows that children who co-view programs with their parents do better in school.

Turn off the TV and don't allow cell phone usage during dinner. Research has shown that children who talk with their parents over dinner get higher grades in school.

Bakan, *Childhood*, 53.
Duffy, *Available Parent*, 2, 75.
Ibid., 4.
Small, *iBrain*.
Steyer, *Other Parent*, 197.
The National Center on Addiction and Substance Abuse, *The Importance of Family Dinners* (Columbia University, 2003, 2005, 2011).

As a parent, you probably already know that too much technology is unhelpful. You might even have strict rules about screen time. But not all rules are created equal. Unfortunately, some rules can actually backfire and fuel tech battles in your home.

Many parents either give up, give in, or use harsh punitive methods.

Rules such as "if you disagree with me, you lose your phone, iPad [or] laptop for a day" might work temporarily. But they don't build trust or nurture your relationship with your kids. And they don't "impart self-control." You may need to use them, but don't use them exclusively.

It preempts more valuable activities such as family conversations and reading, said Pam Withers, co-author of the book *Jump Starting Boys: Help Your Reluctant Learner Find Success in School and Life*, and the award-winning author of 15 bestselling teen adventure books particularly popular with boys.

The below seven strategies, however, can help you set screen time for good without ruining your relationship with your kids. (They're part of an interview that I had with PsychCentral.com in 2013.)

1. Have a family meeting.

"Family meetings promote collaborative problem solving," Gill said. They also help kids feel heard and know their opinions matter to their parents.

Have everyone in the family take turns suggesting possible solutions. Set ground rules, such as no interruptions or insults with calm communication. Keep meetings short, such as 25 to 35 minutes if your kids are teens. You can even set a timer.

2. Let your kids "earn" screen time.

They can earn screen time by doing constructive, creative or charitable projects and activities. For instance, some parents let their kids earn screen time by reading, Withers said. "[F]or every *hour* of pleasure reading they do, they are allowed *half an hour* of media time. This sends a clear message that reading is valued more than electronic-media time."

Gill knows a 14-year-old boy who's earning screen time by creating an original picture book for his 3-year-old brother. She also suggested these service projects: "Entertaining a younger sibling, raking the neighbor's yard, baking cookies for the widower down the street, sorting laundry, or reading to the neighbor's preschooler."

3. Make cutting back a family affair.

Are you constantly on your phone? Does your laptop feel like another limb? Before making rules about your kids' screen time, consider the kind of example you're setting with your own tech use, Withers said.

If you're also committing to cutting your use, she suggested creating a parent/kid challenge: "Pin a chart on the wall with both parents' and kids' names over columns that track screen time."

Another idea is to create a "family electronic-device drop-box at the front door for certain hours of the day — at least for dinnertime.

4. Avoid setting extreme limits.

For instance, don't set rules such as no screen time for two weeks, Gill said. "[It] is difficult to enforce, so the parent is tempted to give in after a few days."

5. Replace screen time with other enjoyable activities.

"[T]hat way you are not focusing on the negative 'you can't' [but] rather [on] the positive 'look what you *can* do,'" Gill said. "But it requires sacrifice, brainstorming with your kids, or letting them experience boredom (horrors!) for a period of time." Note: Boredom leads to creativity.

6. Let your kids pick their tech activities.

Set a time limit for using technology, such as two hours per day, Gill said. ([T]he American Academy of Pediatrics recommends against screen time for children under two years of age — urging more interactive play instead — and recommends a maximum of one to two hours of quality programming per day for older children," Withers said.)

Then give kids the freedom to figure out how they'll spend that time. Do they want to watch a TV show, play a video game or visit a favorite website?

This teaches kids to "pre-plan, and [helps them] feel respected as you help them choose," Gill said.

7. Be interested in what your kids are watching.

"Express curiosity about what's happening on their screens, rather than trotting out judgment and lectures," Gill said. Talk to your kids about what they're watching, how popular it is with their peers and, most importantly, what they think of it, she said. "Teens love to be regarded as experts, especially by their parents, if only for moments a day."

Continuing the interview... all these things are still true.

-- Why is screen time problematic?

The 4 things kids need most is

1) to Connect,

2) to feel Capable,

3) to feel that they are Contributing, and

4) to develop Courage (the ability to handle the stresses of life constructively)

None of these goals is really attained by screen time. Also, it does not develop any of the senses except overstimulating the visual & audial, to the detriment of other senses. Nor does it help with physical exercise. This sets the kids up to be highly susceptible to struggling with stress, as they are neither exercising nor developing their brains.

They need to give and receive from people non-verbally to connect and develop relationship skills. Eye contact, physical touch (example:

SCREEN TIME (FROM JUMP-STARTING BOYS)

wrestling with your son, doing your daughter's hair), and using words are vital to healthy growth.

To develop true self esteem, they need to create, use their talents to contribute, and learn self control.

-- <u>What are the most common obstacles parents face when setting limits on screen time?</u>

Ineffective parenting. Many parents either give up, give in, or use harsh punitive methods, all of these are ineffective.

-- <u>What are the most common mistakes parents make when trying to set limits (e.g., rules that might backfire)?</u>

Lack of relationship tops the list. Rules like: "if you disagree with me you lose your phone/Ipad/laptop for a day" may force temporary compliance but they do not foster relationship, or build trust.

Rather, work with them to let them choose when they will spend, for example their 2 hours a day that they are allowed to use it, so they learn to pre-plan, and feel respected as you help them choose

-- <u>What are effective strategies for setting limits?</u>

Family meetings promote collaborative problem solving. Earning screen time through constructive projects, service projects, work, reading is a good strategy.

It is best to replace the screen time with other activities, such as games, projects, etc, that way you are not just focusing on the negative "you can't" rather the positive "Look what you CAN do..."

-- <u>Anything else you'd like parents and caregivers to know about setting limits on screen time?</u>

Parents must set a good example, and talk to the kids about how they too are committed to limiting their own screen time. One family I know takes a whole day every week to disconnect.

https://www.amazon.com/Jump-Starting-Boys-Reluctant-Learner-Success/dp/B00EV99TQM/ref=sr_1_2?dchild=1&keywords=Jump-starting+boys%3A+Help+your+reluctant&qid=1611892735&sr=8-2

NINE

Voice

"They have to have voice," explained my mentor to me in 2004. She was describing the journey out of an eating disorder for one of our clients. I had never thought of that before. Voice? Really? That set me on a new understanding and appreciation of allowing kids to express themselves. Since then, we have had much experience with teens that are suicidal, and it is not pretty.

Hmmm. Read on, and rethink. "Is it really necessary to be right all the time?"

In 1983, the world lost a talented artist with one of the most beautiful singing voices to heart failure caused by chronic anorexia. Karen Carpenter, in the midst of fame, fortune, a loving family and tremendous success as a singer, starved herself to death.

Understanding eating disorders requires us to understand the need all people have to be heard. In our work with young people we all too frequently hear "my parents do not listen to me. They think they are right all the time." When children and young people have no voice, we see three common responses: eating disorders, cutting (self-harm), and suicidal tendencies.

Sadly, the problem is growing, especially among religious families. When parents have strong religious beliefs, they work even harder at convincing their children to do as they say, to listen to them, and to follow their directives. They are sure they are right. And maybe they are. *But in being "right" they are not effective.* Relationships do not flourish when a person's' voice is not heard. Powerlessness leads to the three things mentioned above, as well as various addictions, which we all hear so much about in the media.

Effective parenting requires empathy. Empathy is only released through listening. Don't you need to know that what you've said is important? Certainly! And so do our kids. An empathetic response is "I understand why you feel that way." Notice it's not "I feel that way" or "I agree with your feeling that way," but I UNDERSTAND.

Active listening acknowledges the emotion behind the statement. Too often we focus on the content of what they're saying and we argue with that. This does not connect with the child's heart, and usually puts both parties on the defensive. Because the parent is bigger, more articulate, and smarter, the parent usually "wins" but in power struggles, who really wins? *Parent, do you want to be right, or be effective?*

I'd like to review the acrostic to describe what young people need that I mentioned in the early part of the book LOVE: Listen, Order, Voice, and Empathy. As Americans, we don't listen! We're more concerned with what WE are going to say next. This needs to change if we are to rise the next generation to be healthy confident individuals.

Order means that they are not in charge. There needs to be someone who can guide them (yes, even kids who vehemently believe they should be in charge, they still need guidance!). But, remember, if parents are too busy to engage with the kids, children will be very discouraged. Use humor to maintain order, it works wonders.

Voice is expressed first by crying when they are infants. In orphanages and homes where babies are neglected they learn early on that their crying will not bring a comforting response. So they lose their voice very early in life. How vital for us to give them that voice back again. Two authors that address the needs of adopted children very well are Karyn Purvis and Heather Forbes.

Empathy is vital when the child is angry! Yet so many parents get emotionally hijacked, and get angry themselves. Stop, back up, apologize, and have a "re-do" when this happens. Your tween and teen will respect you more in the long run.

The answer to our hurting young people is to give them a voice and choices. But be careful, it is risky business! If you are a parent, you will need to spend more time with them, listening, understanding their struggles. You will also need to deal with your own insecurities and hurts from your past.

If you are a youth worker or counselor, the abusers will be angry with you, so they will accuse you of wrong doing. (See Proverbs 9:7,8) In my profession, that happens all the time. We even have an informal name for it: the "Angry Dad" syndrome. Correcting and exposing abusers is not for the faint of heart.

But, if we can spare some families the pain and sorrow that those go through by giving them a voice, it is worth it. After all, we want fewer people like Karen Carpenter, the beautiful singer who had no voice, and more like Martin Luther King, confident and secure.

TEN

"I just want to be happy"

One day I told my granddaughter I had the secret to happiness. I had her attention! When she looked at me questioningly, I said "People who are satisfied with what they have, and don't long for more are happy." (That is number 2 below)

Clients come in and most of them say, "I just want to be happy!" Here are four tips to happiness.

1. **Defeat bitterness**. Everyone has to battle against bitterness, because all of us are hurt sometimes. There is much pain in this world! We can choose whether to let it fester, in resentment, or give up our right to hurt the person back. I know people who hold on to bitterness for decades, and my heart goes out to them. They are not happy! It's a process to **forgive and let go** of things, and one we all need to learn if we want to lead a fulfilling life. Our pastor says, "Time doesn't heal all wounds; it heals **clean** wounds." That is wounds free of bitterness.

This quote was on my son's wedding invitation recently: "Be soft. Do not let the world make you hard. Do not let the pain make you hate. Do not let the bitterness steal your sweetness…" (Iain Thomas)

2. **Be thankful.** The opposite of thankful is **entitled.** You can tell how much "entitlement-itis" is robbing you of happiness by how much you complain. Is a complainer happy? There is always something to be thankful for, and you can train yourself to be grateful. Start by writing down three things a day you're grateful for in a journal (and don't let yourself repeat any). Train your children to be thankful, so they don't fall into the way of thinking that says they're the center of the universe and the world owes them.

3. **Have courage!** Don't let **anxiety or fear** take over. How much of your thinking is focused on the "what if's?" Most of these never happen, but they occupy way too much of our thinking. Try this: whenever you're tempted to think of the "what if's," say to yourself "what next?" Then concentrate on making dinner, or fixing the car, or cleaning out the closet... much more productive thinking than focusing on what you can't control anyway.

4. **Serve others.** People who give to others less fortunate than themselves are infinitely more happy than those who live a self-focused life. That's why people who seem to have it all are many times so discontented. I personally think that that's why God allows disabilities, suffering, and weaknesses: so we have the opportunity to help others. Raising or working with children certainly helps us grow up and get rid of our selfishness.

If we can "fight the good fight" and manage to defeat these four things: bitterness, entitlement, fear, and selfishness, we'll live satisfying and reasonably happy lives.

Let **forgiveness, thankfulness, courage, and selflessness** characterize our lives!

Those, dear granddaughter, are the secrets to happiness.

ELEVEN

Anxiety

"My child was diagnosed with anxiety!" "So was mine."

"Mommy, what if someone steals our car while we're gone? Daddy, is the fan going too fast, will it fall down and hurt us? I'm not sure that we should leave our dog here for a few hours, someone might steal him..."

Anxiety has replaced depression as the Number 1 mental health problem in the country.

We CAN treat it, with intentionality and effort. I use the phrase "Stinkin' Thinkin'" quite liberally (and it's funny enough that it often brings a laugh). Try holding your nose, not saying anything, and if they question you say "Guess what is Stinkin' Thinkin'..."

Here are some techniques to help overcome anxiety:

   a. Change the "<u>What if's</u>" to "<u>What next</u>?" This switches our thinking from the imaginary to the real: from awfulizing to seeking solutions, from the huge, nebulous, fear-filled unknown to the next concrete step we <u>can</u> take. It empowers us and most importantly changes our <u>focus</u>.

b. <u>Our focus determines our experience!</u> What am I focusing on? The negative? If ten people compliment my new haircut, and only one says she doesn't like it, do we focus on the ONE negative?!

c. <u>Choose</u> to believe that "I am not a victim, I can control my attitude about this.

   Although I cannot control other people or the circumstances, I <u>can</u> control my own attitude."

d. When we make mistakes, we need to admit it, and then stop beating ourselves. "I made a mistake, that doesn't mean I have no value, nor does it negate all the good in my life."

   One person said, "There are <u>no such things as mistakes, only lessons</u>." What can I learn from this one?

e. Make it a goal to say at least <u>one positive thing</u> to as many family members & friends as possible, and to <u>yourself</u> each day. (note: Many people will say that they compliment others readily, but seldom say positive things to themselves!)

f. Some people find it useful to limit their worrying to 15-20 minutes a day. Set the timer for say 8:00, then again for 8:15. During this 15 minutes, WORRY, do all the "What if's," and think of solutions to the worst case scenarios. Then when the timer rings, put all the worries back into a Worry Box, and don't worry about them again until tomorrow, at the <u>Worry Time</u>.

   Elementary kids can even make a physical <u>Worry Box</u> that they put their worries in, until Worry Time. This really works! I use it all the time with my clients.

    g. People of faith recognize that ultimately humans are not in control. This is very helpful to remind ourselves if our belief system includes the idea that in all things God works for the good of those who love Him, who have been called according to His purpose. It allows us to <u>relinquish control</u>.

In response to the kids' objections above, I would say, "Now, is that Stinkin' Thinkin' or truth talk? Shall we put that in your worry box? Tomorrow at 7:00 we'll take it out and talk about it.

We can get the upper hand on anxiety! Exchange it for the peace that passes understanding.

ANXIETY

TWELVE

How to Defeat Depression

Depression is rampant in our society, and with the Corona virus, it has risen significantly. Many parents are struggling with depression. Imagine this scenario.

"Kylie, mommy doesn't want to get up today. Can you bathe and feed the baby?"

Mom is asking her daughter to be the parent, because of her weakness. We call these children "parentified," and they unfortunately bear scars their whole lives from it.

NO! Parents need to be parents, persevere, get help, whatever it takes. I always say the best thing you can do for your kids is to get your own emotional pain healed.

Here are some tips to defeat depression. Maybe you can't win the battle totally, but you CAN parent your children. For their sake.

1. *Let yourself be grateful.* All of us can find little things to be thankful for. We live in the most affluent nation on earth and have many blessings that we can say "Thank you" for. Write down three things every day

that are different, some specific, small things, that elicit an attitude of gratitude in you.

2. *Volunteer.* Help at a homeless shelter, make meals for shut-ins, help out at a place for orphaned animals, visit elderly people in a nursing home, rake your 90-year-old neighbor's yard. All of these get the focus off of yourself, and on to someone else. Who has it worse than you. It's guaranteed to make a person feel better.

3. *Exercise.* Even a 15-minute walk will produce some endorphins, making you feel better. However you like to exercise: biking, jogging, dancing, pilates, walking, playing tennis or basketball...choose one and then figure out how you can do it several times a week. It really works!

4. *Write.* Journaling is a very successful way to overcome depression. Somehow, committing it to paper gets it out of our mind and articulates it. That's better than letting it sit in our head and ferment. When I journal, I try to end it on a positive note. An inspirational saying, a Bible verse, a poem. This lifts my spirits.

5. *Read the Psalms.* David was depressed for over half of the Psalms, and minced no words in expressing it. He vents quite vociferously in some places, for God isn't afraid of emotion! But notice, in every Psalm, there is at least one verse thar shows the faithfulness of God. A little light to illuminate the darkness. David knew all about the dark night, the agony of the soul

6. *Connect with someone.* It is the tendency of people who are struggling with depression to isolate themselves. Reach out, even though you don't feel like it! Ask a safe person if you can vent to them. Let them know that they aren't to fix you, you just want their listening ear. Don't stay alone, and it's best not to do it through texting. Face-to-face contact is 100% better.

7. *Pray about it.* I mean short prayers, like, "God, I have lost hope, please

help me." "What shall I do about this despair?" Then expect God to answer you, even if you have doubts

8. *Work on something creative, use your hands.* Knitting, sewing, weaving, making cards, drawing, painting, playing an instrument, baking, cooking, play dough sculptures, beading, making jewelry, woodworking. These are just a few of ideas you can use to focus on something that you're creating, and it feels good!

9. *Cuddle with a pet.* If you have one, your love will pour into the animal, and often it will return to you. If you don't have one, borrow one. Consider getting one, as they are very therapeutic. Or, go to a pet shelter and cuddle with one there.

10. *Educate yourself.* Reading or listening to podcasts about depression may help you to overcome it. There are many books and articles that address it, and do a good job. *Finding Hope Again* by Drs. Neil T. Anderson and Hal Baumchen is a good one.

11. *Try something new.* A new hobby, something that you've never thought of trying before, will distract you, and may give you a new lease on life. Another language (try Duolingo, a free app that allows you to learn languages easily), woodworking, writing letters to prisoners, gardening, any of the things mentioned in #8 above, Befriend a foreigner, write thank you notes to old teachers you liked, get involved with some cause that you feel strongly about.

12. *Smile.* It's scientifically proven that smiling makes a person feel better. It uses less muscles to smile than to frown, and it send the message to your brain that there is something to be happy about. It's also infectious, causing other people to smile, thanks to mirror neurons. Try it!

13. *Ask someone to tell you that this too shall pass.* It might even get better tomorrow. Or next week, or next month. This came from a depressed client, and it makes sense. The distorted thinking one has is that it'll always be this bad. That's never the case.

14. Are you eating *healthy food?* Plenty of protein, fruits, and vegetables. And drinking enough water? Beverages low in sugar, caffeine, and alcohol? How about your sleep? You need to take care of yourself physically to feel good.

15. *Listen to music.* Music stimulates both sides of the brain, and can reach deeper recesses of our soul than talking can. It isn't understood why, (people who have had strokes can sometimes sing, but not talk), but it often works to calm and to encourage us. Have a playlist of encouraging songs ready to play when you get down, and see if they don't work.

If, however, you are seriously depressed, it would be good to *see a professional.* Rather than judge you, the counselor will help you learn some tools to defeat depression. It's worth a try! 5 sessions could well be all the person would need.

A word about *medication.* I believe that anti-depressants are God's gift to us, but are to be used sparingly. If a person is very depressed, they might need something to get them back up to feeling decent again. But rarely should the medication be seen as a permanent solution. You need to change your thinking to get well and stay well. Medications in many cases (but not all) are like the scaffolding on a house that is being built. It's there for a while, but not long term. Changing one's thinking, figuring out and beating the distortions, is how one builds the house.

You CAN overcome depression! Many people go through it, and come out the other side. You will too!

THIRTEEN

On Children Leaving the Faith

"Mr. Jones, this is the police. We have your son here; he was arrested for possession of marijuana..."

"Mom, I'm pregnant..."

"Dad & Mom there's something I have to tell you, I'm gay."

"You force me to go to church, and now that I'm 18, I want you to know that I am an atheist and will never go again!!"

Nothing strikes fear, guilt, and grief into a parent's heart like hearing that their child has chosen to turn their back on our cherished beliefs. When they embrace a lifestyle that we not only don't agree with, but also have spent all of their childhood years trying to inoculate them against, many parents sink into despair and say, "How did I fail?" Others may reject the child, cutting him or her off from the family until they repent. In their anger, they blame the devil, blame the church, the pastor, or God. Some even leave the faith themselves.

I believe the #1 reason children reject God is that they feel *shame* when they think of Him. Inadvertently as parents, we use shame to teach them obedience. After all, that's how our parents taught us right and wrong. *Shame is toxic. It can be defined as the belief that "I am bad," and differs from guilt, which says "I did something bad."* When a person feels that they are bad to the core, there is a despair that comes, for we were not designed to live in shame.

Theologically we know that mankind has fallen into sin and needs to be restored to a relationship with God through Christ in order to remove our shame. But all too often we teach our children that that occurs through works, not grace. We can quote Eph 2:8 & 9 backward and forwards but still in our heart of hearts we communicate that a person's acceptance depends on their performance. Why? Because we (emotionally) believe that ourselves! And it robs us of peace and joy daily.

Take our common child rearing practices for example. Jack hits his brother and steals his cookie. "Jack, WHY did you do that?" we cry in distress. Really the only correct answer to this question is "well, mom, theologically speaking, I have a sinful nature, and my flesh got the better of me, I am bad to the core." When we ask a child WHY he did something that is usually a shaming question.

Another error parents make is to focus too much on the behavior and not enough on the relationship. If we are honest, we are really worried what others will think of US if our children misbehave.

An international authority on raising troubled children, Dr. Karyn Purvis, says, "Connection needs to come before correction. Every child needs to know his or her preciousness." (www.child.tcu.edu) Day after day the child gets the idea that he is never good enough, he can never totally win our approval unless he is perfect.

So why would he serve a God that is even more difficult to please? God's way to bring change to lives is through a mentoring, guiding, and loving relationship. *Grace changes people from the inside out, and it is really the exact opposite of shame-based methods we all too often employ.*

I asked several adult children why so many of their peers have left the faith, and got very similar answers. They can be summarized in two words: "hypocrisy" and "legalism." As such an indictment on our spiritual walk, no doubt these words will serve to produce copious amounts of guilt in parents' hearts. But let's look at them.

No one would deny that we make mistakes, but it seems that if our children name it "hypocrisy," they are saying that we are refusing to admit them. Jesus was very blunt with the Pharisees, calling them out on their refusal to admit that they were putting up a religious façade. People who cover up their failures, who put forth a pretentious front are actually covering up their own shame.

I've told countless parents that one of the best gifts they can give their children is to deal with their own emotional issues. We can only reproduce what we are. How can we expect our children to get it about a loving God when we are so filled with shame?

One indication of this is that we always have to be right! When my dad was teaching me to drive, he warned me to be very careful at intersections where I had the right of way. "You can be dead right," he explained. This analogy carries over into relationships. Being "Right" can do more to kill your relationship than many other things.

Legalism is the attitude that we gain our standing with God through following a series of rules. Such performance-based Christianity is taught both explicitly and implicitly in many churches and families around the world. It produces tired, self-righteous, and discouraged people whose concept of God is that He is harsh, distant and unloving. *"Try harder," the leaders, tell their people when they struggle.*

Parents inadvertently pass this concept on to their children, and then wonder why some them choose not to follow Him. Again, the answer is to get our own hearts right with God, to press through past the "Try harder" stage into true grace. Accept God's power and love, cooperating with Him so He changes us from the inside out.

Motivated by love, experiencing brokenness, and receiving His gentle, firm correction when we need it is a far cry from the legalism that our children perceive. We rush around trying to perform to a certain standard, then not admitting it when we fail.

I'd add to this list, a wrong use of power. Some parents, pastors, teachers, and bosses become very enamored with their position of authority. They somehow get the idea that they are infallible, and conduct their relationship with those under them as if they are always right. Pity the person who is spirited enough to challenge them! They will be immediately labeled "rebel", "incorrigible" "not able to receive correction." And dealt with accordingly, which usually involves shaming, crushing, or ostracizing them.

Some pastors and parents conduct an emotional "Reign of Terror" by having this mindset, especially if they are in a system that perpetrates such beliefs. Is it any wonder that 80% of our young people run from the church when they get the chance? Sarah Bessey, popular author and speaker (www.sarahbessey.com) said, "I got PTSD from the church." She along with many others blog regularly about the need to respect the dignity of each person. Abuse of authority is a major reason many youth are launched in to the world wounded, and do not succeed for an extended length of time in pursuing their goals.

Some authorities think that to be abusive, one must be volatile, and display temper outbursts. This is not always the case. I know cases where people in authority were "quiet bullies." They never lost their cool, and prided themselves on it. However, their self-righteousness did not allow them to see other people's points of view, and they took their own authority so seriously that they caused much hurt and division in the organizations they were part of. Many, many young people have been hurt in the fallout created by self-righteous "quiet, calm bullies."

How can parents and other leaders learn to model respect, dignity, and humility?

A few ways I can think of:

1. Listen. Don't always be so quick to speak. Be quick to hear, slow to speak.

2. Learn to disagree respectfully. You can do this if you are not emotions-led, and can respond instead of react. But beware! Emotions often highjack your good intentions.

3. Be ready to learn from your rebel. After all, rebels are pioneers; they have a lot of courage.

4. Empathize that they have been hurt. Even if you don't agree with them (what they are saying might well be outrageous), recognize that they have been hurt. Give them time to sense your love and empathy for them. You can't change them anyway.

5. Focus on your relationship with them. You can have a good relationship with your kids even of you disagree. I know first hand that it's possible! Love is the most important thing.

The scenarios mentioned above are too often a reality for many parents today. We can pray and love them, and find like-minded parents to pray with. The story is told of St. Augustine's mother, St. Monica, who prayed like crazy for years. Look how her son turned out!

It's humbling for us (isn't that a good thing?) and keeps us on our knees before God. I have verses highlighted in my Bible for prodigals. Here are some of them: Is 44:3, Is 54:13, Is. 59:21, Jer. 31:16,17.

ON CHILDREN LEAVING THE FAITH

For decades I have prayed for one of my sons, and I still believe that one day he will choose Jesus. Meanwhile, I love him unconditionally and do not preach at him or try to change him. Love. We can do it. We can rise to the occasion. By God's grace.

FOURTEEN

The Number 1 Reason Kids Reject Christianity

"Mrs. Gill, if you could do one thing differently, what would you do?" A former student asked me this question, and I had an answer for her. "*Listen more. Talk at people less.*" *Show more empathy.* Parents and teachers are notorious for their inability to really listen to their kids, and to show empathy. But we excel at talking AT them. Explaining why we are right.

Micah J. Murray's blog captured my attention because as a therapist, I see it nearly every day in my office. And sadly, in my former career as a teacher I was guilty of it myself. http://micahjmurray.com/why-i-dont-cry-to-christians/ Why doesn't he cry to Christians? The indictment is clear: WE LACK EMPATHY.

Is our inability to empathize due to our arrogance? Head knowledge is seductive, we think that by educating our youth they will suddenly say "Oh thanks for straightening me out on that issue" and change! If we can just convince them of the rightness of our argument, it will have a magic effect on their hearts.

I actually believe that there are other factors involved as well. Our own personal history is a big factor. Many of us grew up in an empathy-free zone; our parents were too busy and/or too hurting to listen to us. Encouragement is in short supply in most families.

But in Christian families, references to God are not lacking. Children and young people may hear Him referred to when they do something wrong, or even worse when their parents are angry with them. So they conclude that He doesn't really care about their hearts either. He is too busy, too righteous, and too distant. "So why would I devote myself to someone like that?" they conclude.

Lack of empathy results in shame. My last blog addressed this, and it is lethal. But rather than focus on the destruction caused by shame (there are plenty of blogs out there written by young people who have rejected the faith that express it vividly), let's look at ways to import empathy into our relationships.

"I'm so mad at my teacher…" Rather than immediately correct our young people for their disrespect, we need to hear their hearts. "Pick your battles" is a common adage for parents and teachers, but we don't really pay attention to it very well. If we did, we'd stop and realize that in power struggles no one really wins. The relationship suffers often-irreparable damage.

How much better to meet their hurt with empathy first. "I hear that you are really angry." Win their hearts! Later, when they are calmed down, is the time to engage in collaborative problem-solving techniques. "What can you do to solve this problem? What will work? What CAN you change? How can I help you?" Better to play the role of *consultant, not the rescuer.*

That is another major reason we lack empathy. We want to solve the problem, and rescue our "poor kids." To fix them. Such an underlying belief is rooted in our own shame. In our haste to make ourselves feel better by solving the problem for them, we deny them the very empathy they need to grow. Young people need to feel our confidence in them. It starts with empathy.

Let's change our paradigm of parenting and teaching. Let's snatch this generation back from the arms of the world, that is often more empathetic than we are. No wonder the anonymous writer of the letter cited above won't turn to Christians anymore for help. Let's not let that indictment be said of us in our families, churches and schools.

Let's slow down and listen, show our youth that our hearts are big because of a huge, loving God. Let's replace lectures with listening.

Save the words for the good times, when hearts are calm.

FIFTEEN

8 Simple Prayers that Help Marriages

Often parents cannot get along. Sometimes, their conflict becomes overwhelming, and they divorce. I left teaching and became a Marriage and Family Therapist because I saw so clearly the damage that broken marriages do to kids. These prayers are designed to be prayed either together with your spouse or apart (or both).

1. **Lord, give us tender hearts for each other and for You.** This is a powerful prayer. It's based on Matt. 19:8 where Jesus says that "because of the hardness of your hearts, Moses allowed you divorce." When we get hurt, we harden our hearts which leads to emotional separation. Pray this daily for our spouses and ourselves! Some days praying this several times is not too often.

2. **Lord, help us to hear You together.** In Is. 30:18-21 we learn that He longs to bless us and that He will direct us. How vital to develop the ability to hear His guiding voice in unity! Pray to "hear" and then tell each other what you have heard from God. Then pray again to choose a course together.

3. **_Lord, what should I say and what should I not say?_** Help me know how much to say, when to say it, and if I should keep silent on this issue. Prov. 15:23 say that an apt answer brings joy. There are many other Proverbs that speak of the danger of using too many words. We need to learn discernment on what is too much and what is "stuffing it" or saying not enough.

4. **_Lord, give me Your eyes to see him/her._** II Cor. 5:16 says we can learn to recognize no one according to the old nature. Asking Him to help us see our spouse with His eyes is very helpful, as our vision is often clouded with our own hurts, preconceived notions, and history of wounds from others.

5. **_Lord, help me see myself as You see me._** Due to our own personal wounds we are often harsh with ourselves. This also causes us to be critical of our spouse and children. Song of Sol 6:9-10 is a precious Scripture that shows how God sees us. Ps.139:13-16 also address self concept issues. One of the greatest gifts we can give our spouse and children is to allow Him to heal our emotional pain.

6. **_Lord, help me to encourage myself._** In I Sam 30:6, David showed that he knew how to encourage himself in God's strength. Too often we rely on our spouse for encouragement, and try to get all our needs met from him/her. As we learn to rely more on God to meet our needs, it will greatly improve our marriages. We will be like less like a vacuum cleaner, sucking the life out of the other one and more like a fountain, overflowing with love to give out.

7. **_Lord, help me to encourage my wife/husband today._** Heb. 3:13 urges us to encourage each other, because life is full of discouraging situations that drain us. How can we be part of the solution rather than part of the problem for our spouse?

8. **Lord, give me victory over bitterness.** Heb. 12:14-17 warns us that a bitter heart can pollute many. Most notably our children will learn to harbor bitterness, resentment and unforgiveness if we do not get victory over these negative emotions in our marriages. "Forgiveness is giving up your right to hurt the person back who hurt you." (Dr. Archibald Hart) This understanding has the potential to change marriages everywhere. After all, a marriage is a union of two good forgivers.

Final Word

Parenting is my passion. As I write this, I have 7 grandchildren, some of which are teens, and several of which are tweens. But even before grandchildren I had it as my desire to help parents and see kids blossom.

How much we have to learn! Yes, we learn from our mistakes, but how much better if we could learn from someone else! Hopefully this book has helped you. Feel free to write me at cynthiagill1972@yahoo.com Tell me what has meant something to you from the book. Tell me what you disagree with. And tell me what parenting tips you have found that work. Perhaps there will be another book which contains them…

God bless you! May the Maker of the Universe and Creator of our kids (and us!) reveal Himself to you in a deeper way as you go along this road.

"He who began a good work in you will carry it on to completion until the Day of Christ Jesus." Philippians 1:6

Resources

Discipline that Connects with Your Child's Heart by Tim and Lynne Jackson

Have a New Kid by Friday by Dr. Kevin Leman

How to Talk So Kids will Listen and Listen So Kids will Talk by Adele Faber and Elaine Mazlish

Jump-Starting Boys: Help Your Reluctant Learner Find Success in School and Life by Pam Withers and Cynthia Gill

Parenting Your Teen with Love and Logic by Foster Cline and Jim Fay

Positive Discipline by Jane Nelsen, Ed.D.

Raising Grateful Kids in an Entitled World by Kristen Welch

The Collapse of Parenting by Dr. Leonard Sax

The Narcissism Epidemic by Jean Twenge, Ph. D. and W.K. Campbell, Ph.D.

The New Strong Willed Child by Dr. James Dobsen

Acknowledgments

I'd like to thank first of all my husband, who in the midst of writing other books, has shown his devotion to me in ways too numerous to count. Love you, sweetie pie!

To my children and grandchildren, thank you for all you've taught and continue to teach me. To my clients and students, I appreciate all I've learned (and continue the journey!) from you guys.

Thanks, Abigail, for your very creative pictures! They're great!

And finally and most importantly of all, I'm eternally grateful to the Lord Jesus Christ, for He meets me every morning and speaks throughout the day telling me "This is the way, walk in it…" (Is. 30:21)

CPSIA information can be obtained
at www.ICGtesting.com
Printed in the USA
FSHW012044080321
79297FS